MY BOOK OF THOUGHTS

MY BOOK OF THOUGHTS

A Blueprint for Breaking Free and Living Your Life Purpose

MARTINA TREER

The intention behind this summary of thoughts is to share my steps of breaking through illusions. (aka the wisdom acquired throughout my almost half a century long life)

The initial purpose for this book wasn't to profit from it, but to help others who might find these thoughts useful in practice.

This book is filled with experiences, stories of beautiful encounters, realizations, a variety of lessons, a plethora of learning, personality-building, and evidence of never-ending growth.

If this book helps only one person, I will forever be grateful for the opportunity to make a difference.

Table of Contents

LIFE – A Gift from GOD

Do you ever think about what life really is?

There are so many possible answers that could clarify this question; I guess it really depends on the point of view. My own look at life is as one of the greatest gifts, a very special school.

Many people are looking at life somewhat as a punishment because of the difficulties they need to deal with on a regular, everyday basis.

To constantly chase daily tasks and anxiously await only for the relaxation time is to consciously torture yourself, which is completely missing life's point.

Viewing life as a struggle is a mainstream opinion that is as far from the truth as it can be, yet it is the easiest and most convenient way to calm one's conscience and avoid putting action to break through.

People tend to fall back into the commodity of daily routine, regardless of how "bad" it is and complain. Let's face it, the acts of complaining and producing never-ending excuses are probably the most popular sports of modern times.

CONDITIONING

Truth to be told, babies are being born perfect and already complete. I was blessed by God to be able to observe it in the example of my own son. They come to this Earth as miracles. The fact that young children learn at the fastest rate is a valid proof of that point.

Children already come with the divine abilities, which are unfortunately being spoiled by sustained conditioning that we lovingly call "raising".

In reality, raising is nothing but just passing "the knowledge" of accustomed ways of living from generation to generation.

Instead of being protected by parents and adults in general, or being seen for who they truly are and supported to become their best selves, those beautiful and unique little beings are being raised by the rules accustomed by generations of ancestors.

These "proven ways" of parenting very often become a not-so-glorious legacy of:

This is how we have lived and survived; therefore, this is the way you should do these things as well.

From the earliest days, kids are being told of what they should and shouldn't do, while their individuality and divine gifts such as intuition and freedom of thought (no matter how different from usual they are) are being censored for the reason of fitting into the golden standard of society.

The reason behind it is that it serves the group of bored people who self-entitle themselves as "the ones who rule the world" by grouping us all in THE AVERAGE, so that we are more rulable.

Please don't ever blame children for the stupidity of their parents; they are the only wealth that really matters in this world.

LOVE AND LOGIC

Logic

I often think of the common ways of doing things and find them completely ridiculous; allow me to elaborate on that in the following:

Firstly, we are born perfect and unique.

Secondly, we work hard to suppress our individuality throughout our school life in order to blend in.

Finally, again, we need to be unique to "succeed" in life.

If this isn't the most illogical and time-wasting way of doing things, then I don't know what is.

Yet, we continue to value logic above feelings.

<u>To be perfectly clear:</u> I am not saying that logic is not important; it does have its valid place, but it can't be applied to everything.

Roughly speaking, logic is relevant to probably a third of all thoughts, but it is not applicable in all life situations.

One of the best examples is seen in the fact that logic is completely irrelevant when it comes to love.

We can see proof of it in many situations, such as:

- A person we love hurts our feelings, but if love is alive, we would forgive them time and time again – Where is the logic in that?

- People mostly judge others solely based on appearance; we often forgive them and try to work on connections anyway – Where is the logic in that?

- You are tired after an exhausting work day, but your child wants to eat pancakes close to midnight, and you go ahead and make pancakes just to see him happy. Again, the question is, where is the logic in that?

Logic doesn't exist when it comes to love.

It never did, and it never will.

If we look at life purely through the eyes of logic, we will always get to the place where it doesn't make any sense. True understanding of life and wisdom lives in the heart.

Trying to find logic in everything leads to overthinking, and subsequently leaves a person stuck going in circles, puzzled and without actions, results or growth.

Love

"Love" – a beautiful word with the most misunderstood meaning.

For a feeling to be called love, it needs to be unconditional - always and without exception. **If it isn't unconditional, it isn't love!**

Love is a gift of the highest frequency and a feeling that should be shared without any kind of expectations or reciprocity.

Everything else that looks similar to it is not love.

People use the famous 3 little magical words without realizing that they often expect something in return with a silent "if", "when", or "therefore" attached to it.

To someone who understands and lives that frequency day in and day out, it is sad to see people misusing this word while being convinced they are talking about love, while ultimately robbing themselves of ever feeling the real thing.

My advice:

Love immensely, without expecting anything in return, and please don't ever punish new people in your life for the bad experiences you went through with people in your past.

By doing that, you might just miss the most beautiful gift God wanted you to receive.

True love is never a sacrifice, a transactional deal, a commodity or a convenient codependency.

Love is unconditional; it shows us the interconnectedness with ourselves as well as with everyone in the world because we are coming from the same source, and no one can ever deny that.

My look at anatomy:

LOGIC – BRAIN

EMOTION – HEART

INTUITION – SOUL

My advice:

Invest in yourself by continuously working on acquiring the following, and growth will not lack.

Head – Rock Solid

Heart – Wide Open

Soul/Spirit – Always ready to go

FAMILY

"Family" – the term that I see as a representation of the most sacred union; a word which I associate with the highest purpose, connections, warmth, coziness, loyalty, an everlasting constant, a safe place in the world, and so much more.

Some lucky people on this planet were blessed to get families which are worthy of that name. I will not be talking about those.

Unfortunately, in so many cases, families as unions lost their purpose and exchanged it with sole actions behind titles, as if these were corporations.

The titles (mom, dad, uncle, aunt, cousin, son, daughter, wife, husband, etc.) are very often owned by their members as the right to exercise their ways of seeing you as a walking ATM, always available pro bono psychiatrist, or just a number they can dial at any time they feel the need to dump out all of the daily frustrations while expecting how you don't have anything else to do. They see it as your duty to always be the available shoulder to cry on.

And so, little by little, you are being lured into the web of someone else's stories, gossips, life riddles, and problems that are preoccupying your mind.

And why is that?

Because you care, you are kind, you love them, and only naturally - you want to help.

Years go by, life happens, and you are automatically available to everyone until you find yourself in a situation in which you could use some help as well.

Of course, you don't ask for it because you are independent, you were raised to be strong, resilient, and you can do it – it is expected that you can do it alone.

At the end, you indeed do it, you do whatever needs to be done, you go through the challenging times by yourself, while all of your beloved family members go silent as bears in hibernation.

Suddenly, everyone is busy, everyone lays low and waits for troubling times to pass because, after all, you are the strong one, you always know what to do, you'll manage.

Inevitable gossips behind the back are running 24/7, and sometimes, on those rare occasions, if they decide to comment on your situation in front of your face and cordially ask if they can help, deep down, you know it was offered with the intention for you to politely refuse.

What comes next, you ask?

Very predictably: you just do it, you do whatever needs to be done, always, without a doubt.

But what also happens is: you start waking up, gradually, understanding what is going on, but still finding excuses for your family, people whom you love the most in the world, people who love you, or at least they should be, by definition.

If you are really brave, if you dare to doubt, you start testing the situations here and there and find yourself in disbelief of how far some of the members can go, and all of it just because of the jealousy, for the need to keep you under control, to live off of your energy. And all of the above because they choose to neglect the needed work on themselves.

Oooooh..., the skills of manipulation are amusing and terrifying at the same time, and all cloaked with the veil of good intentions.

A friendly suggestion: Please don't ever approach a person with any but pure intentions, and *especially* not with the "good for you" ones.

What happens next?

You are sad for a bit, then you probably start thinking how you are exaggerating because... It's your own family after all, and very soon you find yourself in the situation of overthinking.

You go in circles of forgiving, being hurt, aggravated, being reactive, being called crazy or too much and then exhausted again.

This makes up the cycles of your life up until one significant day – the day you decide to choose yourself.

That particular day happened to me a couple of years ago. I was walking out of the bathroom where I potted the palm trees and caught myself looking directly at a photo of me taken in 1983. in the garden of our vacation house by the beautiful Adriatic Sea.

I immediately remembered how I felt in that moment, when my grandma called me to stop playing with the plants and pose for a minute. I am so grateful for that. And although I have a serious face, as my son commented, "Mom, you look like you were solving the world's problems!" I remember how happy I was.

In the very moment of looking at the photo, I felt like my life flashed backwards all the way to that day and how my brain half-consciously scanned all of the situations in which I neglected that child in me.

From that day on, I decided to protect that little girl first and foremost, to regain my life back and to live it as intended.

So, the day you decide to choose yourself is the day you choose to take a long, hard look at your life; you choose to stop excusing everyone around you and understand that your life without everyone else's interference is actually beautiful.

At the same time, you are also realizing how all of the things that were bothering you and all of the things you were so passionately trying to resolve are actually other people's problems.

This is the moment that marks your wake-up from all learned beliefs. This is the moment from which you will choose yourself and never, ever look back. The moment in which you dared to climb the first step and started your journey of ascension.

Keep in mind that the process will feel like you are transitioning worlds, changing timelines or stepping into the new realm. Everything you once knew will feel completely different to you, and that's ok, just keep pushing forward.

Remember that **YOU are NOT the problem**; those are the lies coming from the ones who can't bear the light you carry in your soul.

And don't forget to congratulate yourself because it took tremendous courage to unlearn everything that was being indoctrinated in you, and an immense strength to proceed with your own path of living in your true purpose.

My Advice:

When thinking about the past, focus on the happy moments.

Life is beautiful, don't waste it.

Love and Integrity Live here

SELF LOVE – SELF ACCEPTANCE

The fact that you chose to distance yourself from others and work on yourself doesn't mean you are punishing people, but simply that you have finally learned your lesson – you have passed your test and you are being allowed to start the new cycle of life.

The highest love of all is indeed pretty easy to achieve; learning to love yourself is the way. While walking that path of challenges, and believe me, there are going to be many, you can always find your readily available strength in the love you have for yourself – this is your God-given superpower.

Don't be afraid of the risk of change. Risk sounds scary, and the purpose of its meaning is to keep you stuck in the same place. Risk is just an illusion that is worth taking to follow your dreams and make them come true. Mine is to always try to follow what my heart knows, and God's is to show me if that is the right way for me at that moment.

Duality is existent in everything; One can see the same sentence in two different ways, for example, from the light point of view: "Rise Together", or from the more shaded point of view: "Rise to Get Her". All of us have two sides, and for the sake of this chapter, let's call them the light and the dark side. The topic here is not about being good or bad; it is about the balance, and about what one is actually using their dark side for. If it is being used as a protection of your light, it is very beneficial. Strive to have that duality balanced at all times. Lead with light and have the other one ready for the case of protection. Don't be afraid of encountering darkness; it will help sharpen your vision.

Keep coming back home to yourself.

Regarding everyone you are distancing yourself from, my favorite teacher (He knows who He is) would say "Love them anyway" – He is being more gracious than me. I, on the other hand, will always Love them despite! (Meaning: I will always love them unconditionally, but without being affected by their intentions because I <u>accepted</u> the situation, <u>forgave</u> them instantly, and <u>allowed</u> myself to heal.)

RELIGION

I don't mix Faith with Religion. I respect all religions as long as they don't harm living beings; I find them interesting and inspiring. So many people found faith through religion, and I respect that. Religions are bringing diversity to this world.

Throughout life, I have been learning about different religions and experiencing different places of worship for the sake of education. I was always feeling calm, fulfilled, and most of all inspired after those experiences. It was all because of people and their open hearts.

I always liked to go to church because of the sense of togetherness, the sound of the organ and just a beautiful frequency produced when people are singing together. I have never resonated with the practical part of the protocol, but I have always loved to wish peace to others.

I still go to church when I have time because I love being close to people, but I also have a direct connection with God.

God is within me every day of my life, and I nurture that relationship. As for the other guy, we have a mutual respect – I don't deal with him, and he doesn't touch me.

FAITH

I make sure to touch up with God every day.

I don't necessarily pray for hours or sit in silence for long periods of time because I am simply busy with different obligations, but I am consistent, I always make sure to say thank you to God and the Holy Spirit, to ask them to protect all of the good people and pray for the souls of the ones who decided to go with some not so glorious choices.

Life is indeed a magic that we need to become aware of.

It is immensely important to take a deep look within yourself and practice inner hygiene. The process is pretty uncomfortable because if we truly want to work on ourselves, we need to deal with the mistakes we once made, confess them to ourselves and find the strength to apologize to the ones we wronged while forgiving ourselves in the process.

Nevertheless, it is very important to ask yourself if you are fulfilled, content, and what it is that you really want from this life.

Personally, I don't want to just exist; I want to fully live my life. I want it all, and somehow, someday I will achieve it; I simply know that in my heart.

You see..., people are often using so much time for strategizing, laying out plans for how they are going to make things happen, and I agree that it is important to have a solid mental sketch of what it is that you are trying to achieve, but you really don't need to know all of the steps beforehand.

Life itself doesn't function like that. Overthinking and over-strategizing leads to self-doubt and self-sabotage, meaning the goal is very rarely being achieved.

My advice:

Think about what you would like to do. Make a mental picture of it, allow yourself to feel the feeling of it and make a decision to take the first step.

When your thought, your feeling, and your decision to go for it align, the only thing that is left to apply is your commitment and your consistency.

From then on, success is inevitable.

PAIN

Pain is such a cool teacher if one is open to learn. It is hard to go through it, but it is so rewarding. If one is open to working on themselves, results are never absent.

So please take one step at a time, but choose yourself each and every single day.

Let pain pass through you, not to you. Allow yourself to grow, to become sharper, stronger, resilient and unstoppable in achieving your life's purpose.

When experiencing situations in which you feel you have been betrayed, cheated or ghosted by the ones you deeply care about, always remember that they didn't cheat you; they actually cheated themselves with the opportunity to continue being in your life, and they usually figure that out way too late.

I had a chance to go through a situation of being betrayed by a close person at the time:

One of my friends from the neighborhood decided to steal my gold credit card while I was at her home visiting her for a coffee and a talk. She did it out of jealousy and thinking that it was so cool to go to the store and purchase things by using it. She made a huge bill, and we eventually ended up in court; it was a whole mess, but little did she knew I had that card only for the case of emergency and not for spending around – I was never raised in that manner.

Another example was a family friend from childhood who boldly decided to use my first and last name to give it to one of the main characters in her television series.

The same female character was sleeping with her boss in the second or third episode of the show. I knew the moment I saw it, I would have a very interesting week at work with all of the murmur behind my back. It was yet another mental exercise.

For someone who was completely committed only to one person my whole life, this was the act of a major disrespect, but the saddest thing is that this friend from childhood actually thought she was doing me a favor portraying my name through a "bad ass" character, like it was a huge achievement to be climbing the corporate ladder through physical exercises. I am not judging others; people have the right to do whatever they want with their lives, but this is something that I am not aligned with – I never was, I never will be.

And always remember the bad guy's "bad ass", no matter how fabulous it looks, is always and without exception subpar to the "God's Cool one."

My advice:

On your path of growth, there will be many known and unknown people with many opinions.

Take their point of view into consideration and stop there; don't seek for their validation. Validations are only feeding the EGO, and that never ends well. Know that acting in ego is projecting you as a villain to the world around you.

Step back, assess what you were suggested, go within and allow yourself to see if it resonates or not, and then just proceed accordingly. You will save yourself so much time and confusion.

Take the stored grief, anxiety and pain, and transmute it into something beautiful. Utilize the depth of the feeling gifted by pain, flip it and use it for creation.

Validation of others is not needed.

While we can always learn from others, on your path of growth, you will encounter unnecessary drama, emotional vampires and energy siphoners. People will try to stop you in your path because your growth makes them uncomfortable.

Be aware, it will never feel like they are wanting to control you (especially when it comes to close ones to us), it will feel like loyalty, but in reality, they will be trying to take control over your actions back into their hands.

Don't seek for validation or approval, do not care to impress others, and never bend to manipulations. Refuse to be controlled, choose your own authenticity instead. These are the perfect situations to respond with logic instead of warmth.

In here, choose to make a SHIFT. This shift is called clarity - empathy without reciprocity, meaning: allow yourself to understand the thoughts of others and where they are coming from when offering advice, but without expecting from them to understand you. Just simply regain your energy.

People might misunderstand you, but you will always know who you are, as you understand yourself. Be in alignment with your true self, be authentic.

Speak kindly, move slowly, walk in grace, and be grateful for people who are now a part of your history.

My Advice:

Ask yourself: "Do you have the courage to set boundaries for everyone you love, regardless of the intensity of the spiritual bonds, to show appreciation to your own self?"

Choose self-love, because only then you will be complete and ready to love another person the right way.

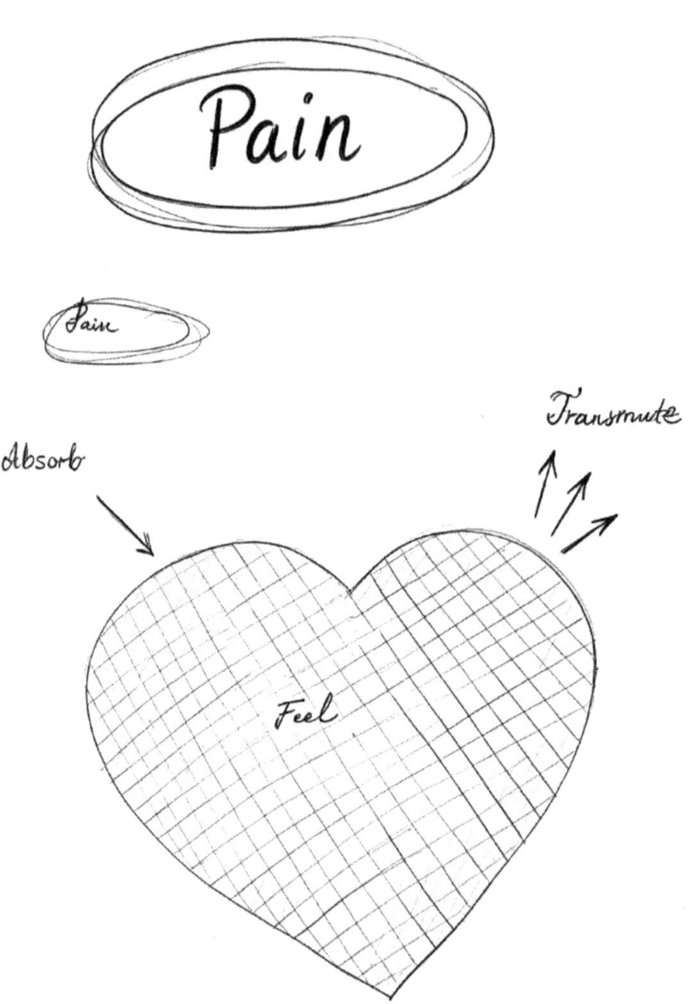
Pain
Pain
Absorb
Transmute
Feel

PEOPLE

I love people.

Whenever I have time, I enjoy a cup of dark, bold espresso on my local grocery shop terrace. Just sitting in silence, enjoying the sun and observing life happening around brings me joy. It is amazing how many signs and synchronicities are happening around us at all times, and the majority of people are unaware of them.

They are missing the magical part of life.

People are walking around preoccupied with their own thoughts – I find that sight beautiful. If they would only stop for a moment, live in it and understand how simple life really is in the reality of things.

Each person is unique, carrying so many stories and experiences within, each one is a real-life walking library. Very often, they are drawn to me, and we start talking. Almost always, those unexpected talks end up being the best and most inspiring ones because they are unrehearsed, and being made without expectations, just as real and genuine as life used to look when we were kids.

My advice:

Whenever you feel drained, or sad, or just not quite right, make yourself go out.

Be among people, observe and share a smile. That one simple smile that doesn't cost anything might be the only nice thing that someone experienced in a day.

You never know how far-reaching the positive impact your simple smile can have on someone else's life.

SMILE OFTEN AND SMILE MORE.

COMMON SENSE

As much as I try, I can't understand the logic of the common ways, the lack of synchronicities between what people are saying and what they are actually doing.

Ooohh, the audacity of me acknowledging it often ends in comments of how I am not normal, followed with questions about what I am expecting.

"Am I normal?" is the question I often think of.

Well, probably not, and it really depends on what we consider to be the Normal, what is the standard based on which we measure the normalcy of things?

I mean, if everything that is happening around me is normal, I will probably sign off that I am not, but I am very sane; I am very grounded and logical when the situation calls for it.

What I also know is that I think differently from what the standard is.

As just a basic example, here is one simple question that comes to my mind:

"Why is everyone having business meetings on Mondays?"

I know, the answer to the question is probably: "Because everyone does it, it is something that is normally being done.", but I am not everyone, I am me, and this is what I think of it.

It doesn't make any sense to me to have meetings held on Mondays, when people are still under the impression of the weekend and not really wanting to listen to what needs to be done at that particular moment, and also at that point in time, they are probably feeling tense because the working week has just started.

If one wants to get the best from their employees, one would want them to feel laid back, to enable the relaxing state, flux of ideas and for meetings to flow organically.

I truly believe the best day for in-house meetings is Friday.

On Fridays, people are gradually relaxing, and if nothing else, they are looking forward to the weekend, and so they are in better moods than on Mondays. More importantly, if one wants to be the most effective, one would like to prepare oneself before the week starts, instead of using half a Monday for talking about what needs to be accomplished in the week that has already started.

So, you are basically using 20% of the working week in order to prepare for something that already begun. I simply don't see the logic in that.

My Advice:

While waiting for the Common Sense to return from the way overdue vacation, go to hermit mode and work on your intellect, hobbies and things you are passionate about, so, you are ready to go once the chaos clears, and it will clear - because Nothing lasts forever.

RELATIONSHIPS

In all of my relationships with loved ones, I was committed, I was reliable, dependable, loyal to the T, but I failed to be loyal to myself.

Looking back on my life, I seriously don't know if I should cry or laugh... or maybe both at the same time. When I think about it more closely, I am coming to the conclusion that I was walking through the valley of evil masked with familiar faces my whole life.

Am I the only one who bought a story to do good, be yourself, and go through life really wishing people well?

I always worked hard on anything I decided to commit to, always strived to make my parents, my friends, my community and my country proud.

I now have two of them. I am thankful I had a chance to be born in Croatia, a country that has seen many sets of outer and inner bullsh......ers from the very beginning of its existence - ever since the 7th century, but what it never did, Croatia never ever let anyone break its spirit.

In the moments of its history, when it looked like she was on her knees, bullied and molested, misused and misjudged, not having strength anymore, she would defy all odds, powered by the strength of her heart and proceed to rise time and time again. This is one of the most profound lessons I acquired while growing up, and I will always be grateful for it.

I am also very grateful to the US for choosing me and giving me a chance to learn firsthand about living in a country basically made up of people from all over the world. With that, I got a chance to breathe, a chance to experience the variety of cultures living together and enriching the environment by doing so. Again, I am forever grateful for the opportunity, and I thank its people for embracing me.

I loved and will always continue to love people; there is nothing that anyone can say to make me not love humanity.

In the retrospective of my life path to today, by just observing situations, I came to these conclusions:

If I was good, people tried to find a flaw as if I had some hidden intentions,

If I was reserved, they assumed I thought I was better than them,

If I were open, they would think I was showing off.

Throughout my journey of life, I was always walking minding my own business and often receiving remarks of being too good as if that is the terrible crime, as if my sole existence is a scandal.

If I was dressed nicely, I would give the impression of a gold digger,

If I wanted to help, they thought I had ulterior motives,

If I was working hard, I must have wanted to step over everyone,

If I was investing in myself, it would be seen as a threat to the existing relationships and possible business placements.

And so, ..., it all used to puzzle and bother me in the early days, up until I accepted the fact that whatever I do, however I show, I will always be an underdog.

I embraced it and started loving it.

A lot of time had to pass for me to understand that this really wasn't my fault; it was just the projection of other people's insecurities.

My relationships are now clean cut, and my choices are clear.

I am so far from perfect, but I am consistently trying to become a better version of myself.

In this cycle of life, I came to this beautiful planet in a human form, and I intend to be the best version of it I can possibly be.

My advice:

Please be kind to yourself; it takes time for one to acquire wisdom.

Show respect to everyone.

Not everything needs to be known or done in the NOW.

Slow and steady is the best currency when building a long-lasting legacy.

Move past any obstacles placed in front of you in beautiful ways.

Have patience and nurture it because it builds character, and it always pays off.

INSECURITIES

Why are people so unsure in themselves? Why are they investing so much thought, energy, time and intention to doubt someone else's efforts and not to use it for bettering and actually evolving themselves?

That is one good question.

People have a tendency to compete with each other, which I see as a complete waste of time. No one in this world is you, and you are certainly not everyone else. I mean, even the two loaves of bread in the store made by machine are not entirely identical. Each person is unique and should be working on who they truly are instead of copying others, at least if they want to live a happy and fulfilled life.

I thrive being around people with different opinions from mine. I never look at it as a competition, but an opportunity to learn and grow.

Don't compare yourself with others; to compare is to rob yourself of joy.

Today, I accept the fact that insecurities rule the world, 'cause God forbid that I am genuinely kind, have certain feminine body parts and a brain that can construct two complex sentences, it is being perceived as:

"Oh no, this is not possible, we are looking at the 8th wonder of the world!?"

Not many people in this life recognized that the surface appearance is always accompanied by a fully functioning brain. Not many people will approach and talk to you as an equal. When you encounter those conversations, treasure them. It takes a special person to recognize a special person.

Another wonderful lesson comes to my mind at this time, and it was shared by one of my bosses from about 20 years ago. This highly accomplished and very wise gentleman would call the office to touch up on the daily situation while traveling, and the conversation would always go like this:

"Hello Martina, how are you, how is everything going in the office, what happened with so and so, etc….?," and I would say "Hello, everything is fine, it's under control, how are you?", and here, he would always say something in the line of: "Fantastic, I am in good company!" – this would always be followed with a laugh and my question:

"Are you again traveling alone?" and the laughter would go on together with the confirmation.

What a profound lesson that is. To build yourself to the level where you are happy and in a great company by being alone is something we should all strive for.

First of all, it breaks you free from all of the co-dependencies while building your confidence, and secondly, you stop seeking something or someone else in your life to happen in order to feel fulfilled and go through a nice and pleasant day.

I used to always look at people's potential and, based on that, give them chances. I don't do that anymore. I take potential into consideration only if I see the drive and determination behind it. I am looking exactly at what is shown to me through their actions and making my decisions based on that.

I never, ever leave good people behind, but just give them the time and space they need for themselves.

My advice:

Work on yourself. Invest in yourselves whenever possible, grow and don't rob yourselves of the opportunity to experience your life to the fullest.

Be open to learning, be open to the opportunities and strive not to be in the same place you are a year from now. Growth equals constant and committed work.

49

FEAR

Fear is a perfectly legit human feeling. It comes really handy as an inner signal in dangerous situations.

That being said, while it is useful in those specific occurrences, it doesn't help in everyday life. Quite the opposite, it serves as an obstacle to growth.

Sadly, very often, people are scared of that intimidation, not realizing it is only an illusion; they have THE FREE WILL to decide how they are going to feel at any given point in time, and they have the free will to see clearly how they are being manipulated.

One can always decide to break free from the imposed golden prison of everyday standard living. It is a sad and crazy side of the world, ruled by laziness, boredom, jealousy and low vibrations. Looking at it from a different point of view, at the same time, it is funny, clumsy and just amusing.

We are being projected with an intent to become afraid every day. It comes from the people close to us who are planting seeds of doubt, from the news, from the leaders, bosses, coworkers, or just random disturbed individuals we encounter on the streets.

We are being threatened with the fear of those who desire to rule over our free will. We all know what is wrong with the world, but don't speak up because of the fear of others who seem to be more powerful than us. It is all an illusion; they are powerful because, by backing down, we are actually giving them that same power to use to keep us stuck. It is all a brilliantly orchestrated illusion.

Somewhere, in some hidden luxurious caves, some overblown, aged men with too much money and a lack of ideas, being bored out of their mind are gifting themselves with titles, trying to scare and intimidate people with their shallow techniques such as bullying or forbidden occult rituals, while at the same time they are being smaller than a pea in front of their own significant others when they return home. But they are still trying to rule the world because they are "powerful".

Really?!, I have never seen a movie in which the true heroes are hiding their identities, working from the shadows and not being brave enough to stand in front of everyone, clearly state their opinions and lead by example. For all of those gentlemen, I say, please go back and try to torture your wives the same way you are trying to intimidate everyone else; it would be amusing to see the reactions they would encounter at home if they would only dare.

In reality, these are just people who aren't or weren't being loved properly. They all just need to be loved and occasionally cooked for.

Life indeed is a theater, and we are all choosing our roles in that glorious play.

Do we ever stop and think within our own selves of how really f***ed up is to live an unsatisfactory life, holding all of the frustration inside while pretending like we are living it like it's made of gold and at the same time teaching our own kids the same ways, the same rules, and sell them the same bad script we were once fed with?

Why do people do it? Why, when they know how fake and frustrating it is? Why not take initiative, change the script and go by the saying I was taught by the favorite pathfinder guru ever: "If it's gonna be, it is up to me!"

I put myself in the role of the follower only when it comes to God.

What are we afraid of? Every time I think of this, I am closing my hands, looking to the sun and saying: "Thank you God for making me who I am, I am surrendering to you and will do all that I need even if I was the last standing person on this Earth, just please allow me to continue to grow. I just don't want to be in stagnation and miss an opportunity to explore the depths and possibilities of human potential." I was never a fan of the saying, "I am just a human." It doesn't give humans justice because the power of being a human is monumental.

I hug God mentally every single day; I run to his arms every evening, feeling so much grace for having a chance to do so. "Who am I to say that I am not happy, who am I to complain when there are so many people existing at the same time in incomparably worse circumstances?"

I love my life, and I am so grateful for it.

Life is SIMPLE, not EASY, but just SIMPLE. And yet the majority of people are choosing to make it difficult for themselves beyond belief, just because of the temptations, for which they realize, often too late, that they were not worth it, and in many cases weren't as enjoyable experience as they thought it would be, but those ones usually come with the long-lasting and pretty pricy consequences. And all for what? For 5 minutes of fame and pleasure..., if lucky.

We are surrounded by constant news of cheating, and people continuously changing partners, as if it is a cool thing to be able to do that. I don't see the point. Everyone can do it if they want to; it's not like it is an accomplishment worth being proud of.

Ok, got it, it sells the news, but in the simplest of reality, why is it happening? Do people really feel better? Do they feel cool? How long does the feeling last?

I don't think that the grass is ever greener on the other side, because who one person is with their partner, will probably not be the same with you, whether better or worse.

I don't judge, I am just contemplating on the subject. If one is an adult, one can do whatever one wants, but I still don't get it. I would never mess with another woman's project out of respect for another woman, for myself and a sacred meaning of family. I am smart enough to create and work on my own project, because let's face it, if one is in a committed relationship, one is in a team and the relationship is a project, don't you agree?

My Advice:

Go within, remember who you are by remembering your childhood and choose that light.

Don't hold resentment. Rather than being bitter based on the past, go by:

"I trust you until you prove to me that I shouldn't do it anymore."

Understand that when you choose to surrender completely to God, when you decide to do good to yourself and others, you are actually becoming the Light, the Truth and the Way.

When you let God in, you are protected and untouchable.

A Word on WANTS

Listening to everyone around me, observing how things are being done, I am coming to the conclusion that everything revolves around wants.

And I get it in a way, but things look like they went out of control.

Even when listening to my dear friends who I love very much, I am in awe of how many things people demand to find in another human being, and never stop, breath in, breath out and ask themselves what assets they are able to offer.

Examples of this would be: "I want a man who is a lot of fun, earns well, has his own house, a good car, provides, pays for all of my needs and whatnot, while offering just certain body parts and an occasional home-microwaved meal."

or

"I want a woman who looks hot, is not smarter than me, but caters to all of my needs, doesn't spend much and is at all times at home, while I am using my paycheck as a justification for everything else, including not being present, but using all of the above as a pleasant scenery or a stage setting."

Of course, all of this usually comes covered with a beautifully painted veil of a picture-perfect family.

We all have different wants, and that is ok, but what is also important is to do regular inner checkups, to better yourself when understanding why we sometimes react poorly. It is important to stay humble, kind and courageous to look beyond the surface, behind the different avatars people are trying to lead with and truly **see** them by looking at their heart.

MARRIAGE

Wanting to be with a man and wanting to rule over him with your masculine energy is not going to end well, and the same goes for men who are taking women for granted and pushing them to act from their masculine energy, taking away from their femininity, and not allowing them to be women.

Taking away masculinity from a man is the most unwise thing one can do. Not allowing a woman to feel secure and operate from her femininity is a dangerous sport. Breaking the spirit, ruling over another person, blackmailing with material possessions, or God forbid, children, is the lowest a human being can do to another one. It just shows the sad level of co-dependency and insecurity in oneself. It is sad because it illuminates a lack of work on oneself.

I am so grateful to God that I had a chance to learn a lot from a relationship with my First Husband. I will never call him "ex" because of the respect and beautiful years we have spent together. I don't like that "ex" prefix – it suggests that people are discardable and I love and respect him as a human being too much to ever do that.

Twenty-six years long relationship, 18 years of marriage (Yaay!!! We Graduated!), has taught me so much about myself, others, life, sacrifice and persistence. Everything we have we did ourselves; it wasn't easy, we moved 14 times, 5 of which across the Atlantic, each time thinking that it was the permanent one. Going back and forth, working hard and always striving to be responsible and growth-oriented.

We have faced numerous challenges, and many of those were projected to us from our families and their "good" intentions, but we managed to go past every single one of those. If you ever told me we would divorce one day, I would never believe it. But people grow and want different things, and sometimes they don't align. What we never ever did was compare each other with other people, and I am very happy for it, because I look at that kind of comparison as very degrading and offensive.

In retrospect, I am not disappointed in marriage nor love; I actually feel quite the opposite. I will always be grateful to him for being a pretty challenging coach and the most reliable friend I could have ever gotten. I am grateful for our amazing son, whom we both love very, very much. Most of all, I am proud of us for being able to travel this portion of our lives together, learning a lot and still loving each other enough to want to see us happy, even if it means pursuing different paths.

We learned all of the lessons we could from each other, and I know, the same as he knows, I will always have a friend who will have my back in case I need it and vice versa.

My advice:

If love and mutual respect are present, do everything you can to work on a marriage, especially when kids are underage. If it doesn't work, please find the decency inside yourself to part ways as friends.

Love
I've got you
I love you for who you are
We'll figure it out together
Moving with purpose
You inspire me
You are my safe place
Action–Reflection
I am proud of you
I want to build future with you

A Quick Lesson on FEELINGS

Try to look at things more from a feeling level. What do you feel in your heart? If you look at life purely through logic, you will always be puzzled; it will always seem that there is no sense in the particular situation, or that something is missing.

There is a divine plan for a person's life. This plan includes health, happiness, abundance and perfect self-expression.

When focusing on and thinking about the divine plan, you are actually attracting ideas, opportunities, events and people who are meant to be a part of your life's path.

The thing is that people usually overthink situations; they strategize to come up with the exact step-by-step plan of how to achieve it, and don't realize that in that process, they are actually losing time.

The Universe doesn't work like that. You don't have to know the exact steps of how to achieve your goals; you don't have to have it all figured out at the very beginning.

Instead, rely on the divine plan and:

Feel it in your HEART

Imagine it in your MIND

Determine it with your INTENTION

When your HEART, MIND and DEDICATION are aligned, you CAN NOT fail.

Just start living it and proceed from there. Build your faith up, establish a direct connection with God and the Holy Spirit and let all that is meant for you unfold in its own Divine Timing.

What if you don't know exactly what the purpose of your life is or what you really want to dedicate it to?

Think about the things that make you happy. Return to your childhood in your thoughts, remember who you are. Start consciously thinking of your divine plan daily, and it will start revealing itself naturally.

Let go of all things, situations and relationships that don't do good for you and let God in. Free yourself from expectations, and the rest will follow.

A helpful thought:

Remind yourself to let go of the remorse and allow God to show you the way forward.

The path of transformation is going to be simple, but very far from easy. Be sure to be prepared for that amazing CHANGE. Be ready to receive all that you asked the Universe for.

Recognize – Don't resist or resent – just surrender and embrace the journey meant for you.

Please always know that you have everything you need to unfold your best life already in you.

ABUNDANCE, TEMPTATION and a couple of other things

Surrounded by the world being in constant pursuit of happiness and instant gratification, I seek PEACE.

Peace of mind and peace within the heart will produce happiness as a side effect.

It is similar to money.

I was never impressed by other people's money or possessions. I respect their accomplishments, but it is just not relevant to me. I never strived to be seen in the company of specific people - for me, people are who they are and not what they have, just as simple as that.

I never chase money. Don't get me wrong, I do love money as a very useful tool to do great things with, but I don't chase it. I chase knowledge and passion in what I love to do, and money always comes as a side effect.

When we are on the topic of money, or material assets, it is very important to find balance in life, because money comes and goes, but if it is the only thing we value or are focused on, it puts us in a very risky position, looking from the standpoint of the bigger picture of life.

An example from a couple of years ago comes to mind. An investment made in a new virtual type of way. It was a very interesting process to go through, to learn from and to be put in a position in which one needs to choose how to carry themselves with the situation. Intuition was on point, and the investment grew 900% (yes, you read it right, nine hundred percent in the course of about 7-8 months). The enriched worth of the investment was a substantial sum with which one could buy some land or a part of an apartment. And so, the day came when the log in was made through the most reputable page with the most wonderful risk security, but the page had troubles that day, it was hacked and what happened was 1 minute of staring to the screen, watching in real time how the numbers go backwards in a perfect order way back until they reached a beautiful round zero.

And one couldn't do anything about it. I don't have to tell you that no one was to be held accountable, even when the same site stated officially that they had a situation with the page going down that day.

While others around me were out of their mind, pulling hair, and in disbelief, I just sat there. I remember the feeling perfectly. I just sat there and smiled, thinking to myself, who else can say they went through this experience and actually were grateful for the lesson? I really, really was. While that money could have helped so much at the time, it was shown to me that this wasn't the right way and that the plan is something completely different. Two weeks from that occurrence, the amount of the initial investment came back to us in a completely unexpected way, so basically, we haven't lost a thing we owned before, but exercised the intuition and gained a valuable life experience.

People strive to be seen and, in that effort, while being tempted, they very often either lose themselves or find themselves stuck in an illusion. For example, I always smile a little when I see guys peacocking in the fast and flashy cars, because what they are trying to achieve usually goes wrong. First of all, people who are watching are not watching them; they are watching the car and imagining themselves in it. Rarely will anyone ever remember the person who is actually sitting in the car. Secondly, they are putting themselves on display as prey for the others that will usually use them only for their material wealth, so, bottom line, if they are not really enjoying the fast drive for themselves, that purchase was a pretty expensive sport.

People also show off with titles. Titles are so misused nowadays. I respect them, but I don't bow to them. I respect the work and effort woven into earning them, but at the same time, these are worthless if they are not followed with the real, useful and more than anything, readily applicable knowledge.

ASSUMPTIONS

People assume all the time, not realizing how dangerous that is. For example, a wrong assumption doesn't give one a second chance in combat.

While assumptions are pretty challenging and tiring for the individuals who are at the receiving end of them, at the same time, they can be pretty humoristic as well.

An example of my workspace comes to mind. Well, I decided to decorate a space behind my working table with a beautiful print of a hundred-doll bill printed on a black and gold crystal glass. Whenever I am on a call with people who can see me on a camera, I have a chance to observe many different initial reactions, everything from raised brows to a laugh. And while they last for only a second or two, they are very memorable.

Some people are bold enough to comment, ask, or assume the idea behind the choice. In 99% of the time, it breaks down to thinking that I value material the most. It makes me smile. The real reason behind the choice is the person on the bill. He is one of my favorite people from history. When you take a closer look at his face, you will see a slight smile of a person who knows something that everyone else perhaps still doesn't realize.

Besides that, I love the fact that he is one of the rare ones who didn't have **_the title_** of the head of the country, while his portrait is still the one included within the most iconic bill ever. On top of it all, he was an inventor as well. It blows my mind and makes me happy at the same time.

Your knowledge, authenticity and integrity are the only things nobody can take away from you.

VULNERABILITY

Contrary to the popular belief that being vulnerable is showing one's weakness, in reality, vulnerability is a gift and a display of tremendous strength.

Very seldom would one encounter a person who leads with their open heart, showing the real them. A person needs to be genuinely strong and sure in themselves to be able to do that. If you are ever lucky enough to meet someone like that, please acknowledge it. God is great. He sent a friend just like that into my family's life exactly when we needed them. We were lucky because with him came his beautiful wife, who was always genuine and strong enough to be able to nurture a connection with another authentic woman. (Unfortunately, not many are able to do that because of insecurities). Our friends are a beautiful couple, and I love them both very much.

Beware of the flattery; it doesn't bring people far with me, but at the same time, be sure not to dismiss people who are genuinely offering you a compliment.

Intuition comes in very handy here. One of the nicest compliments I ever got was from a neighbor who later became our family friend. He took time from his work to be present at my citizenship ceremony - the last step one has the honor to go through before becoming a naturalized citizen. The compliment shared was that this union became even better, and this, coming from a person who chose to have a profession in which his life was on a display for the benefit of the country, just makes it even more special. Thank you, dear friend, for the beautiful soul you are. I will never forget it.

A Brief Thought on CONNECTIONS

People are often trying to attract individuals, situations or things that are actually not right for them. Don't ever force people to stay in your life; it will bring no good to you. If connections don't come naturally, those individuals are not the right match for you.

If you need to fight to get someone, be sure you will need to fight continuously to keep them. That right here is NOT LOVE.

And when you choose a person, make them actually feel that, rather than making them feel like an easier option.

I had a chance to witness the massive spiritual warfare attempts this year on my own skin. It's not a joke, the thing is real, but what they didn't know is that the Ones close to God are highly protected. I am experiencing episodes of wholehearted laughter lately. Maybe those charmingly amusing idiots finally understood that needling a cloth doll doesn't work on me, so they started tickling it.

To all of the people who decided to project their negativity toward me this year, whether through thoughts or rituals (no need to mention names, you will recognize yourselves) - **I want to thank you for your service from the bottom of my heart.**

Without your help, I wouldn't have flown as high or as fast as I did, but I want you to know I genuinely loved each and every one of you and will continue to pray for your souls.

To all of the good people:

Don't chase the closure, accept the situations you can't change, don't waste your time and allow yourself to sleep in peace, to wake up in purpose, and to walk in the light.

Live your life to the fullest, and if you can do one single thing to make an impact, show up with courage, shake off the anxiety and build a legacy for the future generations, so that the beautiful children who are coming after us don't have to go through the same rabbit holes we once went through.

About the Author

Martina Treer is a highly skilled professional with a background in corporate world, sales and marketing. Martina holds a Master degree in Law, she is a Certified Holistic Nutritionist, Certified Business success Coach, Certified Life Coach, as well as Certified NLP Practitioner.

She is passionate about education, children, veterans, natural healing, biodynamic agriculture and most of all humanity and good in people. This book is a result of her wish to serve with her life experience and knowledge in helping readers to achieve their goal of health and happiness.

Thank You for taking the time to read my creation, which resulted from what others projected is going to be my downfall.

May Light always shine on your path!